The John Danz Lectures

THE JOHN DANZ LECTURES

Nothing But
Or Something More

JACQUETTA HAWKES

UNIVERSITY OF WASHINGTON PRESS

SEATTLE & LONDON

Library of Congress Cataloging in Publication Data

Hawkes, Jacquetta (Hopkins) 1910-
    Nothing but or something more.

    (The John Danz lectures)
    1. Progress—Addresses, essays, lectures.
I. Title. II. Series.
CB155.H36   301.24   72-6150
ISBN 0-295-95231-8

The John Danz Lectures

I<small>N</small> October, 1961, Mr. John Danz, a Seattle pioneer, and his wife, Jessie Danz, made a substantial gift to the University of Washington to establish a perpetual fund to provide income to be used to bring to the University of Washington each year '. . . distinguished scholars of national and international reputation who have concerned themselves with the impact of science and philosophy on man's perception of a rational universe.' The fund established by Mr. and Mrs. Danz is now known as the John Danz Fund, and the scholars brought to the University under its provisions are known as John Danz Lecturers or Professors.

Mr. Danz wisely left to the Board of Regents of the University of Washington the identification of the special fields in science, philosophy, and other disciplines in which lectureships may be established. His major concern and interest was that the fund would enable the University of Washington to bring to the campus some of the truly great scholars and thinkers of the world.

Mr. Danz authorized the Regents to expend a portion of the income from the fund to purchase special collections of books, documents, and other scholarly materials needed to reinforce the effectiveness of the extraordinary lectureships and professorships. The terms of the gift also provided for the publication and dissemination, when this seems appropriate, of the lectures given by the John Danz Lecturers.

Through this book, therefore, another John Danz Lecturer speaks to the people and scholars of the world, as she had spoken to her audiences at the University of Washington and in the Pacific Northwest community.

Preface

As over a year has passed between my delivery of this lecture and its going to press, there is justification for the addition of a Preface. If I may use an archaic image, a considerable amount of water has flowed through the mill since May, 1971, and it may be of interest to see what matter has been ground out.

Comments on the lecture itself have inevitably been few in the period before its publication. Those that I have received have been highly favourable for the good reason that I sent copies of my text only to those in general sympathy with my point of view. I was, nevertheless, particularly glad to win the approval of Professor W. H. Thorpe, the well-known ethologist of the University of Cambridge, whose thinking has led him to favour holistic and hierarchical ideas and to the conviction that 'both subjective and objective concepts are necessary in the scientific study of life'.

Undoubtedly the comment that has given me the most pleasure is one reported by a correspondent from the University of Washington. After my address a student wrote 'BRAVA' across one of the posters announcing the lecture. It seems that my closing remarks about nothing-butism and the younger generation may have found a warm response.

One criticism reached me from an anthropologist who judged I had been unfair in what I said about Professor Grahame Clark. In his opinion Clark's outlook does not differ essentially from my own, for 'he doesn't for a moment doubt that there is "something more" but wants to go further and show how and why this is. . . .' I have known Grahame Clark since student days and readily agree that he is by no means a narrow reductionist, although recently he may have been too eager to see archaeology rigged up in scientific fancy dress. My argument was not directed against his characteristic position, which I greatly respect, but against the particular thesis he put forward in his *Aspects of Prehistory*, the idea that neo-Darwinian laws of natural selection can usefully be applied to the development of cultures and civilizations.

During this same past year, it is sufficiently relevant to record here, I have become an established champion of old-time humanist values in archaeology. As a free-range individual with no academic eggs to break, I have responded several times to the BBC's invitation to stand up to the New Archaeologists with their models and systems and faith in statistics. I ventured far into the lions' den when I went up to Sheffield for a broadcast debate arising from a research seminar, 'Cultural Change, Models in Prehistory'. There I found myself opposing Professor Lewis Binford. To me his long, long abstractions were almost without meaning, while to him I must have appeared as something out of the rotting woodwork.

The debate concerning reductionism of course continues ; there is to be a conference on the biological aspects of the subject at Geneva this autumn (1972). Meanwhile English publication of *Chance and Necessity* by the eminent French molecular biologist, Jacques Monod, has served as a poker to stir the fires. Monod makes brilliant use of recent genetical discoveries to support a philosophy as closed and as dogmatic as any in theology.

The mutations producing the variations on which natural selection works have been shown to be due to chance errors in the DNA code, so that we have 'pure chance, absolutely free but blind, at the very root of the stupendous edifice of evolution. . . .' Having extrapolated this randomness on to the whole universe, he claims that this view 'is today the *sole* conceivable hypothesis, the only one compatible with observed and tested fact. And nothing warrants the supposition (or the hope) that conceptions about this should, or ever could, be revised'. At the end of the book the meaning for man is stated : 'The ancient covenant (between man and nature) is in pieces ; man at last knows that he is alone in the unfeeling immensity of the universe, out of which he emerged only by chance.'

From these quotations *Chance and Necessity* appears as a work of extreme reductionism. It has been accepted in this sense by most reviewers, who have praised or demolished it according to their position in this great issue. Indeed, noticing how often those in sympathy with the pure reductionist aspects of the book wrote with satisfaction of its 'cruel', 'austere' and 'rigorous' judgements, I was reminded of what I said about a possible sado-masochistic tendency among people of this mind. At my most flippant I have wondered how far our differing interpretations of the known facts of existence are related to personality types. The reductionist attitude would go with puritanism, of course, but also possibly with the irrational superiority felt by those who prefer black coffee to white, a savoury to anything sweet.

In fact, however, Monod has not maintained the bleakness of his monody for human hope. On the contrary, he has let in all kinds of moral and other values through his doctrine of the 'ethic of objective knowledge'. More surprisingly, he admits that 'brain and spirit are ideas no more synonymous today than in the eighteenth century', and although objective analysis shows that this sense of duality is an illusion, it is one that can never be dispelled or lived without—'And besides, why should one have to? What doubt can there be of the spirit within us?' he suddenly exclaims, and goes on to celebrate the richness of the inherited soul.

Some of the more purely scientific criticisms of *Chance and Necessity* are equally relevant here. Professor Thorpe pointed out briefly that in accepting neo-Darwinian natural selection through chance mutations as a sufficient picture of life and the universe, Monod has scorned or ignored many serious objections that have come from fellow geneticists and others. Gunther Stent in his full discussion of the book in the *Atlantic Monthly* entered further into these objections, calling attention to the fact that during the last few years some evolutionary biologists have been convinced from their findings in the molecular structure of proteins in living organisms 'that natural selection cannot have played the all-important role attributed to it by Darwin'. One of the troubles with absolute objectivity is that it can give us such various answers.

When I read *Chance and Necessity* myself, I found to my great satisfaction that it contains passages, not mentioned in any reviews I have seen, that appear to support my own speculations about Noam Chomsky's innate structure of language and C. J. Jung's archetypes. Monod considers it likely, and in no way objectionable, that a basic universal structure of language should have been imprinted in the brain during evolutionary time and become in this sense 'a part of human nature'. From language he goes on to allow that other symbol-making tendencies (epigenetic programmes) are similarly an innate inheritance of the brain of *Homo sapiens*. Indeed, here is the origin of Monod's idea of soul, in which we can 'recognize the complexity, the richness, the unfathomable depth of the genetic and cultural heritage' of mankind.

It seems to me that this concept is very close to the ideas of

Jung, who never interpreted the evidence he discovered for a universal archetypal form in more spiritual terms than these. He, too, supposed it to be inherited from our evolutionary past—even if he occasionally speculated about other possible directions.

Certainly the occurrence of such passages of thought as these in the work of a great molecular biologist seems to ensure that Chomsky's prophecy that questions of intrinsic intellectual organization 'will dominate research in the coming years' will be fulfilled also in realms far outside linguistics.

One way and another *Nothing But or Something More* has fallen, as a very humble contribution, into the midst of a tremendously vital, profound, and promising field of research and related philosophical debate. I only hope that the hierarchical organism that bears my name, whether it was created by chance or by a kind of purpose beyond our comprehension, may hold together long enough for me to learn which way the argument is going.

Nothing But or Something More

THE invitation to deliver a John Danz lecture came to me as a most pleasurable surprise. No one could fail to find pleasure in being unexpectedly summoned round half the globe to an intellectual and social adventure. For certainly to come to a great university community on the lovely verges of the Pacific, and to be invited to address an audience on almost any subject, is such an adventure. Both the pleasure and the sense of daring are enhanced by the fact that I am following a procession of Danz lecturers of the most dizzying distinction.

Perhaps I should not have said that I have been invited to speak on almost any subject, for it is laid down that the Danz lecturer should be concerned with 'the impact of science and philosophy on man's perception of a rational universe'. However, for me that generous directive covers every subject that I could *want* to talk about, if the idea of the rational is not too narrowly drawn.

Here already we are encountering a conviction that will be implicit in my whole lecture. If the definition of what is rational is narrowed beyond its true meaning of the reasonable until it excludes subjective experience, a great part of what it means to be a human person, then we are forced into a betrayal of all that is most distinctive of our species.

I have come to have a distrust of the contemporary worship of 'rigorous objectivity' and the withdrawal of the personal even from humane studies. In my own subject, for example, I have urged that excavation reports should not be deprived of descriptions of the expedition, the workers, the surroundings, moments of triumph or disaster and other such relevant human affairs. It is quite wrong to think that scientific truth will be better served by treating that highly social and individual operation as though it were a manipulation on a laboratory bench. The chief result is to make the reports repulsive to all but the specialist. That perhaps, unconsciously, is the purpose.

After this avowal, I hope that you will understand why I intend to keep to a personal style in this lecture. I have said

3

that one of the pleasures in being invited here was to be thought worthy of joining a line of eminent predecessors. I have an association with the very first of them, with Sir Julian Huxley, that leads me directly into my subject.

It may perhaps reassure you that I have no antiscientific bias, if I declare that I come of an impeccable scientific background. That is why I have known Julian Huxley since I was a girl—and on the kind of family terms that lead to frank speaking. In 1954, in a book called *Man on Earth*, I was bold enough to say that I could not believe that the evolution of life on earth was exclusively the result of natural selection working upon random variation. Soon afterwards I was hit by a broadside from Julian. He wrote, to summarize, that I showed unforgiveable ignorance, arrogance and impertinence in my puerile questioning of neo-Darwinism.

Later on, however, when the Huxleys were staying with us, we had an amicable discussion, and after I had managed to produce one or two of the more scientifically based difficulties in the doctrine, his whole attitude changed. He paced up and down my room in a state of emotion asking 'But if it's not natural selection working on random variation, what can it be? What can it be?'

I think it is fair to say that this change was due not to my undistinguished arguments, but to the fact that Julian Huxley is in some ways a man divided within himself. He not only reveres his brother, Aldous, but shares some of his tendencies towards mysticism. Then again, he has always been a field naturalist as well as an evolutionary scientist. He has a passionate love of animals and even of plants, a native and unquenchable sense of awe and delighted wonder at their complexity, perfection and beauty. In fact, if it will carry more conviction to lapse into jargon, he may have a great knowledge of genotypes and their analytical study, but his deepest feeling is for the phenotype, the whole and living individual creature. Thus while he keeps his faith in the doctrines derived from Charles Darwin and his own famous ancestor, T. H. Huxley, he can never be happy with the

4

narrower, colder views of positivism, behaviourism and the general 'nothing but' view of the universe to which they have tended to lead.

Now of course Julian Huxley was perfectly right to accuse me of ignorance and impertinence in writing as I did in *Man on Earth*. My arguments were mainly a mixture of intuition and 'common sense' of the kind most rightly deplored by science. Today I blush at one or two of the points I made. Yet in general I do not repent, for there is at this time a growing school of thought, involving many disciplines, that natural selection working on random variations is only one part, and probably not the leading part, of the evolutionary story. I have spoken of a school of thought, but it is in fact too widely scattered and unorganized to be described in this way—which is probably why it has made so little impression on the general thinking public. It may in fact be all the more significant for this diffuseness and present lack of organization, for it may represent the beginning in one of those great shifts in basic assumptions, in the direction of thought, that prove more fully revolutionary because they are unplanned.

This change in assumptions, then, is particularly well represented by a symposium held at Alpbach, in the Austrian Tyrol, during 1968. It was attended by highly distinguished biologists, geneticists, neurologists, psychologists, psychiatrists and students of linguistics from this country and from Europe. The name of the very remarkable book made up from their papers and discussions is *Beyond Reductionism*.

This title, and notice that it says *beyond* and not *against* reductionism, represents the negative pole of my lecture—that part of it summed up in the *Nothing But*. Reductionism, of course, refers to the scientific method of investigating our world, and gaining control of it, through breaking down its vast complexities into smaller and smaller parts. The superhuman power won by this method is well symbolized by our control of nuclear energy, its brutalizing dangers by the threat of nuclear destruction. In the one direction we can see

5

ourselves as Zeus holding the thunderbolt, in the other as returning to Old Chaos with social, mental and perhaps ultimately physical atomization.

The analytical approach has had such astounding successes in the physical sciences that it has produced an equally astounding hubris among the smaller-minded scientists. What was really a method, one way of turning our brains upon limited aspects of the universe that has produced them, has tended to become a view of life, a totalitarian ideology. It has been held that nothing that cannot be measured and proved experimentally has any validity. Extreme, and I think we can say extremely naive, forms of behaviourism and positivism have captured able minds. Philosophy has been castrated, metaphysics made a dirty word.

Looked at in terms of *being*, reductionist thought suggests that the whole is no more than the sum of its parts and so leads to an old-fashioned mechanistic view. Applied to man this kind of thinking can still produce painful crudities. For example, that man 'is nothing but a complex biochemical mechanism powered by a combustion system which energizes computers with prodigious storage facilities for retaining encoded information'. Looked at in terms of *becoming*— that is within the dimension of time, reductionism suggests that the evolved form is explained by its origins, the fruit by its roots. This reduction to origins can be stopped at any point that pleases the reducer. A vast reading public was apparently delighted to be reduced to Desmond Morris's *Naked Ape*. Or, if we prefer it, we can go back to the assumption, to paraphrase, that there is nothing in man which was not first in the amoeba.

At this point I should like to make a brief aside that is relevant to my theme though not of it. This is the question of the effect of the scientist himself, his psychological type and competence, upon his findings and interpretations. I have already introduced the subject in what I said about Julian Huxley. I grew up in a nest of scientists, and yet I remember feeling rather shocked when one of them assured me that a

6

scientist's research work was always subtly influenced by his temperament and experience.

First of all there will certainly have been a process of self-selection. Many different types of men and women are attracted to the various sciences, but they will be broadly different from those who are drawn rather to the arts and humanities. Among them the finest will have the imaginative, intuitive powers that enable them, as Sir Peter Medawer has admitted, to leap ahead to frame those bold new hypotheses that can afterwards be tested experimentally. Scientists of this calibre will never be crude reductionists, for they cannot forget that this method is only an abstraction from the fullness of life. But they are always a small minority. The average scientist is liable to be practical, an admirer of efficiency and soon to become deeply entrenched in his speciality. Such a man is very ready to forget the fullness of life, to see it projected in his two dimensional world, fixed like a butterfly pinned out on the collector's board. It is so much easier to study that way than when it is flitting among the flowers. Then there are the external pressures, which may be greater than we realize. In the final discussion at Alpbach, a venerable American scientist rejoicing in the degree of unity that members of the symposium had attained, said 'there are so many things that fall into place, if one is careful to avoid doctrinaire prejudice, and avoids acting the way one usually does in one's own guild, where nobody in modern society dares to step out and to speak his mind as we have done in this interdisciplinary group, where none of us gets jobs from the other, and nobody has to worry'. If you feel like that at the top, what is it like when you are far lower down?

Then again I am sure that there are historical-cum-psychological forces that still favour the nothing-but attitude. After all only two generations ago there was still strong religious and ordinary conforming opposition to scientific views in general and evolutionary ideas in particular. The opposition may have been silenced by now, but many scientists still feel it's up to them to belabour it, and they may even take some sadistic pleasure in denying the old values. Medawer speaks of the 'cruel austerity' of the behaviourist method. They are unholier-than-thou boys. Something of the same psychological inheritance inevitably manifests itself in the thinkers who have interpreted scientific reductionism. I would say, for example, that Bertrand Russell quite certainly grew up with a desire to shock and that there was an only partially modified urge of this kind in the young A. J. Ayer. One way and another the pressures to believe, and to teach, that 'Man's perception of a rational universe' must be a reductionist, nothing but, view are still very strong.

Returning now to the changing ideas represented at Alpbach, I can only give the very broadest summary. First, against the basic methods of reductionism one has to set the universal reality of hierarchy. From molecular chemistry upwards existence is structured on this mode, and at each level the parts are, as it were, two-faced, each organizing the smaller ones below and being organized by the larger ones above. At each level, too, there emerge new properties not present in those below. Each organism, hierarchically controlled in this way, is able to maintain itself in space for an appreciable time. In other words I stand before you a specimen of that highly self-conscious type of organism, *Homo sapiens*. You will not expect me to disintegrate into my molecular or atomic parts before your eyes, although that is liable to happen within the next decade or two. Through my brain, I—and here, of course, I am ignoring one of the greatest problems of all—am able to relay messages down level by level to wag my toe or, more audibly, to wag my tongue. What makes this hierarchical system of control over billions of molecules, and this maintenance of the body of your Danz lecturer even more remarkable, is the fact that these molecules are in a state of continual flux, while the cells of my brain are at every moment dying in pale hosts. The great physicist Erwin Schrodinger tells us that he was forced to the conclusion that 'I . . . which is to say every conscious mind that has ever said or felt "I", am the person, if any, who controls the "motion of the atoms" according to the laws of nature'.

This may all seem very obvious to innocents like myself and many of you, but it is a thesis that has to be established every step of the way in the face of the reductionist view of the universe as a thing of physical forces, and mentality as a mere by-product of those forces. It is satisfactory to have been shown that this can be done at every level and experimentally as well as theoretically. The immense importance of this proof of the universal validity of hierarchies is made plain when we remember that so considerable a theorist of scientific thought and knowledge as Sir Peter Medawer has said 'We still seek a theory of Order in its most interesting and important form, that which is represented by the complex functional and structural integration of living organisms'. Here is good reason for biological humility.

Going on from these purely biological ideas concerning organicism to consider such mental questions as learning, thought and language, somewhat related concepts emerge. Simplifying, I think it is right to say that these all tend to demonstrate the inner structural forms and positive activity of the individual living being. Even if the extremes of behaviourism have been for some time discredited—fantasies such as Watson's that thought was derived from the twitching of the larynx—the general notion that the organism is outer-directed, merely responds to external stimuli—still commands wide respect. It is now being shown by those studying the growing infant and child (and the embryo, too, for that matter) that development goes by inwardly determined stages, a cognitive structure that cannot be greatly affected by any amount of coaching. The child learns when he himself is ready and not before.

Recent trends in linguistic theory, as is well known, follow much the same lines. Chomsky and his associates are, I think, generally held to have disproved the behaviourist ideas on language and shown that once again there is innate

9

tendency for speech in the developing child, that he is someone who, as it were, goes in for speech.

Chomsky ventures further in his suggestion that there is an innate, deep level structure of language inherited by all of us and accounting for certain universal similarities between all tongues. I know that many authorities still cannot follow him so far, but I find the suggestion extraordinarily interesting. So far as I know, no-one has discussed the similarity between this idea of an inherited basis for language and Jung's idea of the inherited archetypal forms, more particularly their provision of a basis for universal myths. The similarity seems strong and genuine. Carl Jung always saw these innate mental forms as elementary structures that were then clothed in the fabric of the various cultures. In so far as I understand him I think it can be said that this is exactly what Chomsky claims. The elementary structure is there in the infant and on it he is able to hang his distinctive mother tongue. Jung has often been said to be unscientific, but this is largely because of his refusal to abstract from life, his determination to try to see it always in all its dimensions. His ideas were in fact founded on the meticulous observation of great numbers of patients, on a profound study of mythology, and at least a wide knowledge of primitive cultures. Jung wrote 'It is a great mistake to believe that the psyche of the new-born child is a *tabula rasa* in the sense that there is absolutely nothing in it. Inasmuch as a child comes into the world with a differentiated brain, predetermined by heredity and therefore also individualized, its reactions to outside sense stimuli . . . are specific'. He then said of these '*a priori* formal conditions of apperception', 'They are the archetypes which blaze a definite trail for all imagination and produce astonishing mythological parallels in the images of a child's dreams and in the schizophrenic's delusions . . . It is not a question of inherited ideas but of inherited possibilities for these'.

Chomsky is more difficult to quote since he has to use linguistic jargon and to maintain a proper caution over theories still insufficiently proven. Yet he has clearly committed himself to be essentially a modern descendant of the old rationalist view that the process of learning is in part innate. In accepting the existence of innate human faculties that further the acquisition of language in various ways, Chomsky also commits himself against hitherto prevailing empiricist doctrines. These include the 'conditioning' of Skinner, the drill or coaching of Wittgenstein and the general 'data-processing' typical of modern linguistics. He has written:

'In general it seems to me quite impossible to account for many deep-seated aspects of language on the basis of training or experience, and that therefore one must search for an explanation of them in terms of intrinsic intellectual organization. An almost superstitious refusal to consider this proposal seriously has, in my opinion, enormously set back both linguistics and psychology. For the present, it seems to me that there is no more reason for assuming that the basic principles of grammar are learned than there is for making a comparable assumption about, let us say, visual perception.'
He goes on to end this discussion:

'. . . it seems to me likely that questions of this sort will dominate research in the coming years, and, to hazard a further guess, that this research will show that certain highly abstract and highly specific principles of organization are characteristic of all human languages, are intrinsic rather than acquired, play a central role in perception as well as in production of sentences, and provide the basis for the creative aspect of language use.'

Professor Chomsky was not present at Alpbach, but his ideas were often referred to, and you will see how well they harmonize with the dominant theme that emerged there from so many different disciplines: the idea of the autonomy of the organism, its innate, self-regulating faculties, and, perhaps most significant, its activity and creativity.

I must now return to Alpbach and the subject of evolution. Dissatisfaction with the pure doctrine of Neo-Darwinism was what brought the life scientists together, and it is plain enough that the question as to whether the evolution of life on earth was due to a random interplay of forces, must be fundamental to any challenge to reductionist thought. First of all I think it is fair to make the general point that evolutionary studies in general, and those involving genetics in particular, are at present in such a state of flux that any kind of dogmatism, any claims for absolute certainty, are unwise. There was first the realization that evolution should not be regarded as advancing by lineages, family trees, but by total populations. Similarly and even more significantly, it has been discovered that instead of single genes acting independently to produce particular bodily features, the genes interact with one another in the most surprising ways, so that we have to think of inheritance through the entire gene complex. These and other discoveries have made it plain that living populations of all kinds normally carry a wide range of genetic variations which makes them highly plastic in response to any selective pressure. In other words, the species does not have to wait for a chance mutation to make modifications but can produce them from the existing genetic material.

Such findings lead on to the idea of genetic assimilation associated with the name of Professor Waddington. Waddington has shown that selection can heighten a specific adaptation by favouring genes that make the animal respond more readily and appropriately to stress and the demands of change, a capacity that he calls 'a generalized form of learning'. After some generations of selection the modifications can become assimilated in the genetic inheritence and will appear without the stress. The outward effect of this process is strikingly Lamarckian : the species appears to be inheriting acquired characteristics. The agent, however, is seen as being Darwinian selection—but can we be quite sure what is really involved in this heightening of a capacity for generalized learning?

As well as these large modifications in evolutionary theory, there are, of course, all the new and rapidly developing ideas about D.N.A. Knowledge and theories about the workings of the genetic code change so fast that synthesis and wider interpretations are hardly possible. For instance it has come to light that in two species of *Drosophila* fruit flies so much alike that they can hardly be distinguished, the reiterated D.N.A. is 'astonishingly different'. It means in effect (and there is other evidence as well) that the gene pool can change while the species remains essentially the same—a thing impossible to explain in terms of natural selection.

Then again it has been proved that when living cells are propagated in tissue culture, they may undergo a sudden crisis involving very great genetic changes within a few cell generations, then continue in this new style indefinitely. No one knows what causes the upheaval—but it may possibly relate to a new kind of mutation that could have a large scale effect in evolution. It is no wonder that the leading geneticist, Waddington, himself admits that 'geneticists are at present living in hazardous times', and declares, 'I think we are going to see extraordinary changes in our ideas about evolution quite soon'.

The position can best be summed up by saying that while, at least for the time being, natural selection is still being accepted as the main external agent for determining the relative success of varying animal populations, the nature and origin of the genetic variations themselves are now recognized even by the most orthodox as being immensely more subtle and elaborate than was formerly supposed, and are very far from having been adequately explored or explained. Peter Medawer makes a bald confession when he writes:

'The main weakness of modern evolutionary theory is its lack of a fully worked out theory of variation, that is, of *candidature* for evolution, of the forms in which genetic variants are proffered for selection. We have therefore no convincing account of evolutionary progress—of the otherwise inexplicable tendency of organisms to adopt ever more complicated solutions of the problems of remaining alive.'

Here, then, is a surprising situation in science. Biologists cannot but agree that the living world is composed of organisms ordered at every level on a hierarchical system. It has been agreed for a very long time that the great central current of evolution is that which has swept organisms along through time towards greater and greater complexity. You can witness that we now have from the pen of Sir Peter Medawar, emphatically not one of the dissenting types who met at Alpbach, first that we have 'no convincing account' of how that greater elaboration has been brought about, and second, that 'We still seek a theory of order' for the 'functional and structural integrations of living organisms'. In short, science does not even claim to know how either mice or men have been created in time, nor how, having been created, they are ordered and maintained. These fundamental problems, then, still challenge neo-Darwinism over and far above all the unexpected discoveries concerning odd goings-on in the gene complex—only a few of which I have had time to mention. I repeat, with greater emphasis, here is good reason for humility of mind.

One of the principles emerging from the Alpbach discussions of evolutionary theory was again, as in other related fields, the inner integrity and activity of the organism, characteristics that evidently become more important as one lifts one's sights all the way upwards from amoeba to man. Through its own activity the animal can in a limited sense 'choose' what kind of environment it will inhabit, how it will conduct itself within that environment, and therefore the kind of selective forces to which it will be subject. Waddington gave as an example the fact that at some early point in their evolution the horses 'chose' to survive by running away rather than by standing to fight, and therefore evolved in the direction of fleetness of foot. In an earlier book Waddington expressed this principle very bluntly and with a parenthesis that should interest you. 'We have considerable grounds for believing that mentality in the broad sense, or at least behaviour (biologists tend to be very timid about mentioning the mind), is a factor of importance in evolution.'

This line of thought has been followed further and more eagerly by the marine biologist Sir Alister Hardy. Among all the instances he gives as to how the inner-directed activity, and one can fairly say curiosity, of the animal led the way to evolutionary change, the story of the British Blue Tits is the neatest and nicest. Exploring the caps of the milk bottles that British milkmen leave on British doorsteps, the tits discovered that they could pierce them to reach the milk fat. The information spread rapidly through the blue tit world—an interesting fact in itself. Now the stage is obviously set for evolutionary change in the birds' beaks—a modification that would unquestionably be due to their boldness and mental agility. Sir Alister is a religious man and a whole-hearted dualist, believing that mind and matter represent distinct principles in the universe. It may be felt that he presses the case too hard when he says 'It is, I believe, the mental element in the universe that is the real operating factor in organic evolution ; the constantly varying D.N.A. code supplies the changing material for this selection to work upon'. Perhaps it will be best to leave the last word with the more cautious Dr. Ewer, whose ideas in the strictly evolutionary field have converged with Hardy's. After complaining that the orthodox view on the evolutionary effects of behaviour 'leave out the live animal and concentrates too much on what it is, too little on what it does', she describes various ways in which animal activity can change direction and concludes 'Thus behaviour will tend to be always one jump ahead of structure, and so to play a decisive role in the evolutionary process'.

The point has now been reached, I hope you will agree, when I can claim to have shown that while amazingly little is really understood about the fundamental processes underlying the evolution and ordering of the higher animals, there is a growing body of opinion that mental activity plays an important part. Now it is obvious that the supreme instance of this is manifest in ourselves, the extraordinary species that has created its own environment over the entire earth. Looked at from the hierarchical point of view we can say that the highest step in organization is represented by the human brain-cum-mind. As the essential of the hierarchical idea is that each step possesses capabilities not present in the level below, it is appropriate to put forward full self-awareness as the capability that emerged with *Homo Sapiens*. Self-awareness was, of course, essential to our development of that entirely new and very young attainment of life on earth— culture and civilization.

I want now to move on to the second part of my lecture that will be concerned with this cultural development. It will mean some change of direction, but I like to think that the two parts are firmly strung on one line of thought. At least I shall now be headed towards my own archaeological territory.

I have to begin by taking a step backward to look at the subject itself and its practitioners. A few years ago I published an article called *The Proper Study of Mankind* in which I bravely criticized a school of thought in archaeology which is, in my opinion, being infected by pseudo-science—what I believe you in America call scientism. It is a long time since anything I wrote was greeted with such enthusiasm. I had letters of support from all kinds of people and many parts of the world. Although I didn't think of using the word at the time, I might now accuse this school of archaeologists of practicing an unwarranted kind of reductionism. Alternatively it can be called analytical archaeology after a grim book of that name published not long ago.

I don't want you to think that I am against the use of scientific techniques in archaeology. That would be foolish indeed. Carbon 14, thermoluminescent dating and the rest are most valuable aids—even if their use, and still more arguing about their reliability, does sometimes appear to claim a disproportionate amount of time, energy and other rare resources. What I am attacking is a total approach that seeks

to present archaeological evidence in terms of statistics of one
kind and another supported in every bulky publication by
imposing arrays of graphs, charts, histograms and analytical
tables. In order to strut in this scientific garb, an excavator
may give a whole page of his report to an unsightly histogram
that conveys no more than could be expressed in a single
sentence. Or he may append great flapping tables listing
tens of thousands of unselected flints.

In condemning this kind of thing as scientism, one has to
remember that in archaeological evidence we are not dealing
with universals—all kinds of local and even individual factors
are involved. Nor can anything be established by experi-
ment. In these ways it differs entirely from the data of the
natural sciences. Archaeology is concerned to provide material for the writing of history. That is its glorious justification.
A vast accumulation of minute statistical facts may have no
value at all—no more than, say, an analysis of all the coat but-
tons in this audience according to size, colour and 'profile'.

It is not, however, the extravagant use of academic
resources for a small return so far as the reconstruction of
history is concerned that appals me most, nor even the slight
smell of intellectual dishonesty that arises from this 'scientific' display. Rather it is the fact that if these methods and
this outlook prevail all those elements in human life that are
not amenable to measurement and analysis will tend to be
neglected. We are back, in fact, with the deficiencies of
reductionism at their most extreme, where it is man's self-
awareness and its fruits that are lost in the analytical process.
Religious sentiment, the arts, intellectual adventure cannot
be expressed in graphs, tables and histograms ; moreover to
convey anything about them demands a high standard of
literacy. Better, then, concentrate on technology.

Perhaps I am exaggerating. Analytical archaeology is at
present applied mainly to the Stone Ages, when man's
highest faculties often left little trace. Still, it is spreading,
and already greatly affects the atmosphere in which the subject is taught at some universities—as I was reminded by

several of the embittered students who wrote to applaud my article. How far its assumptions can colour general thinking is exposed in the text of lectures recently delivered at Berkeley and now published in book form. The lecturer was Grahame Clark, professor of prehistoric archaeology at my own old university of Cambridge. His *Aspects of Prehistory* will lead into my discussion of culture and civilization.

Grahame Clark's approach to prehistory has always been scientific rather than humanist, but he has shown a decent concern for human life as a whole, even if he has been mainly interested in its economic, bread-and-butter necessities.

At Berkeley, however, his central purpose was to insist that cultural evolution was a straight continuation of biological evolution and that it, too, was the product of 'natural selection'. 'The thesis I would seek to propound', he said, 'is quite simply that man and his way of life as this has developed down to the present day are both ultimately the product of natural selection.' Later on, conceding that individuals have some significance in cultural development, he remarks, 'An individual man or for that matter an individual mosquito enjoys at any particular moment a freedom of choice limited only by organic attributes and the constraints of the environment. . . . personal dissent has been critically important for the evolution of culture ; it provided precisely the variant on which natural selection could operate. . . . very much as mutations served in the field of biological evolution'.

Here you will detect, particularly in his failure to resist the temptation to put mosquitoes beside men, that professor Clark shows some infection with the nothing-but mentality. What I want particularly to discuss is the thesis that natural selection has been the agency of cultural evolution. To begin with a verbal point, to use 'natural' in this sense extends its meaning so far as to make it in fact almost meaningless. Even on the negative side, cultural selection has often involved purely human faculties : most of all conscious will. It was the will of Cato in particular and Rome in general that caused the destruction of Carthage.

More important from his own scientific point of view, it is surprising to find that Clark made no mention of the fact that if cultural developments are to be regarded as evolutionary then it is a wholly Lamarckian evolution. All kinds of acquired knowledge and skills are, of course, immediately inherited as one generation teaches the next. Now I am no philosopher of science, but in the essential monism of the natural sciences is it permissible for a process to change to a completely different principle in mid-course? I think not. Here I will again appeal to Medawer: after naming the differences between biological and what he calls psychosocial developments, he declares 'The use of the word evolution for psychosocial change is not a natural usage, but an artificial usage adopted by theorists with an axe to grind'. Precisely—and it is the nothing but, the reductionist, axe that is being sharpened. It is sad that so influential a teacher as professor Clark should be this kind of axe grinder, and moreover that he should start trying to apply neo-Darwinism to cultures just when, as we have seen, it is being profoundly questioned even in biological science.

There is a further irony in this situation. Clark expressly ranges his evolution of culture through natural selection against Gordon Childe's ideas as embodied in *Man Makes Himself*. Gordon Childe, probably the greatest prehistorian there will ever be, was a Marxist even though one prone to deviation. He was therefore obliged always to give first place to economics and social structure in his interpretations of our past. Yet in spite of his materialism, he attributed to man an inner drive, a curiosity and energy that enabled him to lift himself by his boot-straps—as is implied in the title *Man Makes Himself*. In this he was far closer to the ideas I have been propounding than is Grahame Clark with his surely retrograde appeal to neo-Darwinism.

If there is something wrong with neo-Darwinism in biology, and totally wrong when it is applied to human affairs, how is it that it satisfies so many gifted minds? The answer seems to be that selection has come to be accepted *a priori* and in that position the principle can be a tautology. As Bertalanffy has said 'Every surviving form, structure or behaviour, however bizarre, unnecessarily complex or right down crazy it may appear, must *ipso facto* have been of some "selective advantage", for otherwise it would not have survived'. Selection in fact has almost been installed in place of God as the given creator of our world.

In the light of these arguments, and others more positive that I hope are still in your minds, let us look at one or two key passages in our cultural history. I will begin with that high hunting age of the Upper Palaeolithic when, some 35,000 years ago, our biologically fully evolved species first emerged—it is thought, though the whole crucial process is still uncertain—somewhere in south-west Asia. According to orthodox evolutionary theory the hunters and their cultural abilities had been brought into being wholly by their competing to survive among other animals on a primeval planet. At least 20,000 years ago and without any change in these outward circumstances, certain tribes living in what were probably very favourable conditions in southern France and Spain, became imaginative artists. Within a short time, in Stone Age terms, they had become masters in brush drawing, polychrome painting, modelling, engraving and carving both in relief and in the round. Among their earlier works were sculptures which I believe can rightly be called religious symbols, expressing their emotional response to birth and fertility. Much of this marvellous work was executed by the light of primitive little lamps in the depths of caves most painfully difficult to reach. In what way can one see these utterly new manifestations of human mentality as products of natural selection? I'm not denying that the animal art did not increase confidence in hunting or that the whole artistic enterprise may not have been good for social cohesion, but note two things. First that the tribesmen who created this first art were not living in highly competitive conditions but on the contrary where abundance of game gave them leisure. Nor did their great creative effort win them success in evolutionary terms. Again on the contrary—their descendants dropped back in the cultural stakes and the next human advances were made elsewhere. I feel very sure that if Palae-olithic art had not been discovered, neo-Darwinians would have ruled it out as a possibility. Indeed, so wildly improb-able did it appear to everyone, that the Altamira paintings were written off as a forgery and their discoverer died con-demned as an impostor by the learned world.

Now let us leap ahead at least 5,000 years, paying no heed to the economic and social changes that went with the begin-ning of mixed farming, in order to observe another period of prodigious mental development : the beginnings of civiliza-tion. Perhaps I should not have mentioned a date, for to-gether with the dawn of civilization in the *Old* World, I want to consider that comparable but later dawn in the *New*.

First of all it is clear that once again the advance to civili-zation began in conditions that were not highly competitive and were therefore not propitious for progress through natural selection if that phrase is to have any meaning at all. The flood plain of the lower Tigris-Euphrates valley had been uninhabited while farming was being developed in ad-jacent upland regions, and its settlement, drainage and irri-gation were undoubtedly deliberately undertaken and wil-fully carried through. In the last centuries of the 4th millen-nium B.C. Sumerian civilization rapidly developed its distinctive form and then maintained it in spite of warfare, conquests and racial change over nearly 3,000 years.

In Egypt the story was much the same, except that in the comparative isolation and security of the Nile valley com-petitive pressures were from the first, and remained, even less. There again, though beginning a little later, civilization shot up to an early climax and was maintained—among the Egyptians with a positive faith in changelessness—through an even longer span of time.

Looking at these two pioneer civilizations, each with so much individuality and going through a precocious youth towards a long maturity and decay, the temptation is surely far greater to liken their history to an organic life span rather than to see it as the competitive creation of natural selection? I think, however, that this temptation, too, should be resisted. Civilization, that creation of the total human psyche, was something new in the world and had its own ways. Analogies, like dogmas, can sometimes be more dangerous than helpful.

There is one other point I should like to make against the Clark thesis before leaving it behind. He says that 'economic competition.... Provided the most important medium through which selection could operate' and then that 'the main drift of evolution in the sphere of economics has been . . . towards obtaining the maximum return for the minimum expenditure of effort. . . .' What an amazing thing to deduce from an observation of our cultural history. Think of the toil of the Palaeolithic artists seeking perfection in their dark fastnesses. Think of the predynastic villagers of Egypt with their flint tools devoting scores of hours to shaping and polishing an elegant stone vase when a pottery one would have served just as well. How these people loved to work at quite useless things when they might have been either idling in the shade or improving their onion plots. Then, later, when irrigation provided an abundance of food, did the Egyptians either rest or improve their technology? Not at all, they cut and lugged well over five and three-quarter million tons of stone and piled it into a pyramid. With any economic natural selection the Egyptians should surely have been eliminated? Nor was it very different in contemporary Mesopotamia, or three thousand years later in Meso-America, although in both these civilizations the wealth and energy were expended on artificial mountains and temples rather than on pyramidal tombs. (And if you can think that we have come so much nearer to that minimum expenditure of effort idea today, need you look further to refute it than to your twenty-foot, expensively decorated automobiles, each carrying one little ego to the office?)

We have heard Bertalanffy complaining that evolutionists accepting selection *a priori* can persuade themselves to recognize any biological feature, however bizarre, as having adaptive value. Clark and others are performing the same feat for cultural extravagancies. Which is more bizarre, the courtship display of an Argus pheasant, or the Great Pyramid of Cheops?

I want now to look more closely at the first civilizations of the Old World and the New from the point of view of my general argument. One is immediately struck by two opposing judgements that offer themselves. One is the conspicuous and significant differences between them, the other the very powerful and fundamental similarities.

We all pay much loving attention to the differences. For me the fact that it is usually possible to distinguish every artifact, however large or small, and say that it could only come from one particular people and one particular period of their history, has always been one of the main fascinations of archaeology. The same diversity must be equally appealing to students of art, literature, religion and so forth. We tend to pay very little attention to the likenesses between different cultures and civilizations – partly because they are less useful to us in our studies and partly because they are easily taken for granted.

Nothing of great import can necessarily be deduced from the similarities between Sumerian and Egyptian Bronze Age civilizations. The Sumerians seem to have inspired the Nile dwellers in their first steps towards civilized life, and there is no doubt that they were in constant communication with one another. It is when we turn to the civilizations of the Americas and their many common features with those of the Old World that we can recognize a fact of profound significance for any understanding of the creative psyche of mankind.

Heaven forbid that I should embroil myself in the long battle between those who believe that the American cultures were native and the diffusionists who believe that they were stimulated by contacts with Asia. I know that sites have recently been found on the coast of Ecuador that suggest

23

canoe loads of folk drifting down from South-east Asia at two widely separated dates. Yet cultural traits introduced by such few, casual and impoverished wanderers could hardly have had much affect on a whole continent. I understand, in fact, that today there are not many authorities who think that the high civilizations with which we are concerned owed any significant part of their achievement to borrowings from the Old World.

It has always seemed to me that far too little attention has been paid to this almost certain truth by those concerned with the nature and functions of the human psyche. It is made more significant by the fact that these American civilizations, and particularly the Mayan, were created in natural environments that could hardly be more completely unlike those offered by the Tigris-Euphrates and Nile valleys.

Surely it was one of the most exciting and illuminating moments in all history when the Conquistadors led by Cortez first saw the Aztec capital? According to Diaz this was on November 8th 1519 'when we saw so many cities and villages built into the water and other great towns on dry land . . . we were amazed . . . and some of our soldiers asked whether the things we saw were not a dream'. And remember that before this, when Montezuma sent one of his nobles down to the coast to welcome the Spaniards, Duran tells us that this man went up to Cortez, 'greeting him and throwing about his neck a gold necklace set with many jewels and precious stones'.

Is it not immensely telling that the representatives of two civilizations created in their worlds apart should meet so easily, find another's manners, possessions, customs and general ideas so little different? It is true that a few moments after the chain-giving, the ambassador caused a laugh by having a meal of turkey and tortillas laid before the Spaniard's horses—but that was a slight practical misunderstanding that only serves to throw into relief the deeper cultural and psychological correspondencies.

Now I intend to bring out those correspendencies by a very crude method. I will present a list of culture traits that appear to have been common to civilization as it was first created in Sumeria and Egypt and civilization as it was later independently created in Meso-America. I will not include those primitive traits already present in late Palaeolithic hunting cultures, nor any of so simple and practical a nature that they are to be expected as a needful response to external stimuli. I will progress from items which involve the common life experience of all mankind and which are therefore relatively poor indicators of possible innate mental correspondencies, towards others that appear to be more and more reliable indicators of this kind.

Dressing the body and especially the head with elaborate clothes, ornatures and jewellery, often as attributes of rank and sanctitiy. Love of gold and silver and their symbolism. Houses of many rectangular rooms with wall paintings, gardens, fountains, and cultivated fruit and flowers. Poetry and music. Organized armies, the taking of prisoners and portrayal of their humiliation. Cities dominated by the monumental architecture of great royal and religious buildings. Worship of an anthropomorphic pantheon immanent in nature and representing natural elements and human qualities, and often with animal attributes. A sun god and earth mother as consorts ; primeval chaos represented by a female monster from whose body the world was shaped ; a divine culture hero. A heaven above and hell below and emphasis on royal and divine rule over 'the four quarters' of the universe. Divine kings in their palaces. Identification of the king with a sun god. Temples for the gods built on artificial mountains or 'high places'. Temples furnished with altars for sacrificial offerings. Animal and human sacrifice. A priestly intellectual élite concerned with hieroglyphic writing, astronomy, the calculation of calendars and mathematics.

The Meso-American civilizations were more precocious than the Bronze Age civilizations of Mesopotamia and

Egypt in having already developed a competitive team game concerned with bouncing a ball and the scoring of goals.

Finally, I think it can justly be said that it was in technical matters that the New World cultures differed most sharply from those of the Old. This was only partly due to environmental opportunities. One thinks particularly of the failure to make practical use of the wheel for either traction or potting and the neglect of metals—to the point that the Spaniards found the Aztecs armed with flint-edged swords. This is significant for my argument, as it is precisely in practical techniques one would expect cultural convergence through common response to external stimuli.

I am very well aware that this plucking of cultural traits from their contexts for comparative purposes offends against the canons of all anthropological schools. However much they disagree on most matters, they could unite in condemning so unsound a procedure. I am also aware that this idea that cultures may be founded upon innate structures within the psyche has a very old-fashioned air. It seems to hark back to those days of long ago when it was quite simply taken for granted that the mind of man was everywhere much the same and liable to produce the same kind of fruits.

I am not at all embarrassed. I would remind you that in the recent past instinct was struck off as a dirty word, but now, thanks to the ethologists, is honourably reinstated. Moreover, many ethologists now think that instincts have been founded upon habits. It has also been proved that species may inherit a part of their behaviour and yet have to perfect it through learning. For example if that charming little bird, the chaffinch, is hatched and reared in isolation he will sing something like his specific song but without the exact phrasing or the final flourish acquired by all chaffinches in the wild. In some other species the inherited element in the song is much less. Similar results have been established for the nest-building methods of birds.

Surely it is to be expected that there is a different but comparable inherited groundwork in human cultural mentality? Such a structure, organization or whatever one likes to call it in the unconscious mind would of course be far more complicated than the inheritance of other species. There would also have to be vastly more variety and flexibility in the forms that could be raised on that groundwork. We are in fact a species with an infinite range of cultural songs to sing, thanks to the symbol-making propensities of our minds. But it seems that the groundwork is there as an inheritance, though presumably one that can and will be extended.

Here we are back with Chomsky and, as I believe, with Jung. You will recall how Chomsky declared of the 'deep-seated aspects of language' that 'one must seek for them in terms of intrinsic intellectual organization' and how he went on to condemn 'an almost superstitious refusal to consider this proposal seriously. . . .' Is not this even more true of the deep-seated aspects of our entire mental and creative life, and has not the recent superstitious refusal to consider it done even more harm to our appraisal of ourselves and to our rational, and I think I can say also instinctive, search for meaning?

Now the main intention of this argument is to reinforce the claim that we are not born with psyches that are blank sheets on which anything can be written by training and experience. It is usually assumed by those who do accept this claim that the inherited mental groundwork, like the inherited bodily constitution, is an accumulation from the past, the accumulation, if you like, of a cultural feed-back. This is assumed in the instinctive patterns of the higher animals and birds which are absorbed from former habits. Chomsky implies it for his deep language structures. Jung says 'just as the human body links us with the mammals and displays numerous relics of earlier evolutionary stages . . . so the human psyche is a product of evolution which . . . shows countless archaic traits'. Yet Jung himself is a little divided in the matter. On the one occasion I was fortunate enough to talk with him. I said I was puzzled that he saw the uncon-

27

scious and its forms as going back through mammals to reptiles, and yet he seemed to find in them an almost superhuman wisdom—it was as though he recognized some little back window of the mind opening on to a greater universe. Dr. Jung smiled and said perhaps he did allow himself to think like that sometimes.

It is probably right to see these genetically inherited mental forms as an accumulation from the past, but I want at this moment to disturb you by making a contrary proposition. It might be called sending up an intellectual balloon, or jumping in at the deep end. The proposition is that these things are given to us not by past aeons but as a process that is unrolling into the future. In other words, that our world, and heaven knows how many others, are involved in a development that can be likened, by one of those dangerous analogies, to an egg developing into a man, an acorn into an oak and so on.

It is a notion I have always fancied—I touched on it in *Man on Earth*. So I was all the more delighted to find that all those eminent life scientists at Alpbach more than once found their interdisciplinary discussion leading them to this idea—and moreover, that they felt free to toy with it because the idea of a basic randomness in the natural process was being abandoned among the physicists and particularly the cosmologists. It came to a head in their final discussion when Smithies said that if one accepted the big bang theory for the beginning of the universe, one usually accepted also that the mass of matter involved was entirely homogenous. He went on 'It is possible that everything was not random to start with, but highly organized, and that this order has been progressively unfolding ever since'. Whereupon Paul Weiss exclaimed, 'That's exactly it. The alternative is open and this has been authorized by the physicists, so to speak. So the biologists may have the courage of their own convictions'. You will see from what I have said about the universals of the first unrolling of civilization, that I should not find it hard to see justifications for the same convictions at that level. What a fine and satisfying conviction it would be, for here would be no historical determinism! We know that at the level of self-consciousness, creative potentialities can be richly fulfilled or neglected, blighted or blocked. Each individual life, then, could contribute to the success or relative failure of the universal process.

It is time to come down from this trip. I have made it chiefly to show how free the movement of speculation remains even for sober scientists once they have advanced beyond reductionism. Like Marx with Hegel, they feel free on the evidence to turn a theory on its head. As Weiss said, 'the alternatives are open'. The idea that has gained such easy currency that the letters D.N.A. and R.N.A. are an Open Sesame to the mystery of life and its mentality is, of course, a tragic, little-minded fallacy.

I will end with a few words about the effect of this long spell of reductionist thought on all civilized societies of this planet, the East almost equally with the West. I agree with the judgement eloquently expressed by Viktor Frankl: it represents the modern version of nihilism — nothing-but-ness in place of nothingness. Here we have the amazing spectacle of men of high human capacity denying those capacities — so bravely built up (or unfolded) during thousands of million years. The more extreme absurdities of behaviourism and logical positivism have died as they deserved among the élite, but they still spread among the rest of the populace. The mind is nothing but a computer, love is nothing but goal-inhibited sex, and so on. And still it comes down even from above: 'Values and meanings *are nothing but* defence mechanisms and reaction formations' some of your value psychologists are saying. It is a kind of belittlement of man that goes with the breaking down of the whole person into little parts and finding nothing human in them; the kind of sub-humanism that sees defecating as being in some way more real and therefore more important than writing a poem.

Yet people cannot really stand it. The will to meaning proves to be at least as essential to us as the will to pleasure or to power, and the psychiatrists are finding that its suppression produces its own neuroses. Most significantly the young can't stand it and are creating, some of them, their counter-culture. They are obviously quite right to turn back to the sadly neglected inner life, to seek to deepen and heighten consciousness. That, rather than production and consumption, is the specific responsibility of man. They are quite right to revolt against the monstrous tyranny of technocracy—a tyranny which has been made easier by our loss of faith in the value of our higher capacities as artists, thinkers, vehicles of religious experience. But they are wrong when they turn their backs on intellect and reason and try to lose themselves in an inner dream. After all the Stone Age hunters did not only go into the cave depths to dance—though dance they did—they also worked hard and with world-changing imaginative power to create an art that is alive after 20,000 years.

Since that time what wonders men have created, what richness and variety we have known! Essentially all I have tried to say to you is that we still inhabit a mystery, and that the best of scientific wisdom recognizes that this is so. Those scientists who live as whole and imaginative men do not believe that anyone has proved that their minds, their individual psyches, are nothing but chance responses to chemical and molecular games played on the skin of the earth. The degraded masochism of this *nothing but* does not represent a rational view of the universe. Let us have the courage to accept the inner experience that tells us that we are something more—and that we may be part of a process that is something much greater still.

JACQUETTA HAWKES was born in Cambridge, England, in 1910. Her father was Sir Frederick Hopkins, a Nobel Prize-winner for his leading part in the discovery of vitamins. Scientists such as Ernest Rutherford, Sir Charles Sherrington, E. D. Adrian, Peter Kapitza and J. B. S. Haldane were part of the everyday scene.

As a young child she was already determined to be an archaeologist, and by great good luck the Tripos in Anthropology was established at Cambridge just in time for her to be the first student to take both parts of the course.

Immediately after going down from Newnham College she joined the famous excavations of Dorothy Garrod on Mount Carmel. Soon afterwards she married a fellow prehistorian, Chrisopher Hawkes, and took part with him in a number of excavations in England and France, while herself doing research into problems of the New Stone Age in Western Europe. They had a son, Nicolas, born in 1937.

With the outbreak of war Jacquetta Hawkes became a civil servant, first in the War Cabinet Offices and later with the Ministry of Education, where she was in charge of educational films until she became secretary of the United Kingdom Commission for UNESCO. In 1949, having published both specialist and popular works on archaeology, she retired from the Civil Service in order to write.

Since then she has continued to produce archaeological books and articles but has been more concerned to use her special knowledge for a more imaginative investigation of human history and its meanings. Her best known books in this field are *A Land*, *Man on Earth* and *Man and the Sun*. She also renewed her relationship with UNESCO by writing with Sir Leonard Woolley the first volume of the UNESCO-sponsored *Cultural History of Mankind*, and subsequently by becoming a member of the United Kingdom Culture Advisory Committee. She has published a volume of poems and two novels and, with her second husband, the author and playwright J. B. Priestley, *Journey Down a Rainbow*. Soon to be published is *The First Great Civilizations*, a volume in J. H. Plumb's History of Human Society series.